# JETHRO and JOEL were a TROLL

**Bill Peet**

Houghton Mifflin Company Boston

LORAH PARK MEDIA CENTER

to Tansy

*Library of Congress Cataloging-in-Publication Data*

Peet, Bill.
Jethro and Joel were a troll.

Summary: Jethro and Joel, a two-headed troll, goes
on a rampage through the countryside.
[1. Trolls-Fiction. 2. Humorous stories] I. Title.
PZ7.P353Jg   1987       [E]       86-20879
ISBN 0-395-43081-X

Printed in the United States of America

Y   10   9   8   7   6   5   4   3   2

Once upon a time there was a gigantic two-headed turnip-eating troll named Jethro and Joel who lived in a pine forest high up on a mountainside.

Since the people in the valley far below never ventured up into the forest, no one but the birds, rabbits and squirrels knew the huge monster was living there.

Their life was simple as could be, with nothing to do but clear the weeds out of their turnip patch every day—and they could have lived there happily forever if Joel hadn't been so grumpy and miserable.

"*This* is no fun," Joel grumbled. "A horrible monster like us should be out rampaging around the countryside, stirring up trouble."

Joel even grumbled in his sleep after they settled down in their cave at night, while Jethro stayed wide awake and worried. He knew that Joel would keep on grumbling until sooner or later he finally had his way.

"I'm fed up!" roared Joel one morning. "No more puttering in the turnip patch for me! Today I'm going on a rampage, no matter what!"

"If you must," said Jethro with a sigh, "then go on your rampage. The troll is all yours for today. But remember, *just* for today, and that's all."

"One day is plenty!" chortled Joel. "Whoopity Doopity!!" Off down the mountainside went the gigantic troll with wild-eyed Joel in full control. He was eager to make the most of his day, and he kept the troll going at full gallop all the way down to the valley.

Joel was hoping to meet a mob of riled-up farmers armed with pitchforks, ready for battle. Then he could have some fun and show off the enormous brute strength of the troll.

But one glimpse of the huge monster lumbering across the fields sent the farmers and all their animals into a wild panic. In a frenzy, they went racing helter-skelter to find a safe hiding place. And in a twinkle and a trice there wasn't a living soul in sight.

When Joel found the farms all deserted and no chance for a battle, he was furious.

"Come on out and fight!" he bellowed. "Come on out, you ninnies!! You little twerps! You yellow-bellied pip-squeaks!!!"

But none of the insulting things he thought of could bring anyone out. The farmers were hiding in their cellars with their families, and they had no intention of facing the huge troll.

In a red-eyed, snorting fury Joel went tearing around the countryside, uprooting scarecrows, squashing pumpkins, and kicking over haystacks.

But after his rampaging all through the morning and into the afternoon the only one who dared put up a fight was a feisty little red rooster.

Jethro, who had been no more than an unhappy spectator, finally spoke up. "Why don't we call it a day? There's no one on earth foolish enough to battle a monster as gigantic and frightening as we are."

"An army of knights might give us a battle," said Joel, with a devilish grin. He had spied a towering castle across a meadow just a stone's throw away.

"This ought to stir them up," he muttered, as he seized a huge boulder in their powerful paws and with a mighty heave sent it flying straight for the castle.

There was a thundering, resounding "BOOM!" as the boulder smashed into the castle wall, and two towers tumbled into the moat. For a minute there was stony silence, and it seemed as if the castle was deserted. Then, suddenly, heads appeared at the windows and people were shouting, "Monster! Monster!! Look! Look out there! There's a horrible monster out there!!"

Then, to Joel's delight and Jethro's dismay, out across the drawbridge came all the king's men on their snorting war horses and with
their lances aimed straight for the troll's huge belly.

"We're done for!" cried Jethro, "we're done for! And it serves
you right!!"

And they *would* have been done for if the troll hadn't been quick as a
twenty-ton cat.

In a flash, the monster dropped flat to the ground, and all the knights and horses went flying topsy-turvy over the troll's huge back, ending up in a heap.

Then, before the knights knew what happened, the troll scooped them all up in one big bunch.

"Ho! Ho!" chortled the joyful Joel. "Now look who's done for! Now who's gonna make a big splash?!!"

And he was about to toss them into the moat when Jethro rebelled.
"No! No!" he shouted. "We can't drown 'em! We can't be that mean!!
No! No! No! Enough is enough! You've had your day!!!"

FLUMP!!! The huge troll suddenly slumped to the ground, and all the knights and horses went sprawling every which way.

Then Jethro shouted toward the castle, "HELLO IN THERE! COME ON OUT EVERYBODY! WE QUIT! WE GIVE UP! WE SURRENDER!!"

"Are you sure?" called the king from a window of his wrecked castle. "Are you sure this is no trick?"

"No tricks," replied Jethro. "No fooling."

Then the king with his queen, followed by armed guards and members of the court, came trooping over the drawbridge; and as they approached the troll the king said, "I hope you are both aware of the penalty for damaging royal property."

"No," said Jethro, "but we'll be happy to pay."

"Good," said the king. "Then it's off with your heads!!"

"Oh no!" whimpered Joel. "NO! NO! That's too much!!"

"He's right," said Jethro. "That *is* a bit too much. But maybe we could even things up by repairing all the damage if someone will just show us how."

"It's a deal," said the king, and he called for his royal architect and master castle builder. "Fabian! Fabian!"

Pretty soon Fabian, a bearded old fellow, came doddering over the drawbridge with a bundle of castle plans and spread them out for the troll to see. Then Fabian explained every detail of castle building, how the timbers and crossbeams fitted together and how the stonework was done.

Since two heads were better than one, the troll learned quickly, and within an hour Jethro and Joel were busily rebuilding the walls and tumble-down towers they had demolished.

With no need for ladders or scaffolds, the giant troll worked amazingly fast. All they needed was a few men to mix the mortar to cement the stones together, and in just three days' time the castle was completely restored. Then the crowd that had gathered to watch the gigantic construction worker gave the troll a tremendous ovation, praising them to the skies.

"TERRIFIC TROLL!!" they shouted. "MAGNIFICENT MONSTER! TREMENDOUS! FANTASTIC!! STUPENDOUS!!!"

Such extravagant praise was too much for Jethro and Joel, and it all went to their heads. They were so proud of their newfound talents that they decided to make a career of it.

From that day on, Jethro and Joel were master castle builders. They traveled about the countryside building castles for just about everyone. Since the troll had no use for gold or silver, they were paid with a big sack of turnips, and at that price even the poorest of families could afford a castle.

So it finally could be truly said throughout the land, "Every man's home is his castle."

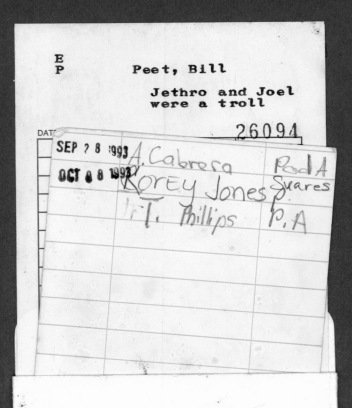